Structuring Information: Internet Energy Intensity and Efficiencies Volume 3

𝕴𝖓𝖘𝖎𝖉𝖊 𝖙𝖍𝖊 𝕮𝖆𝖘𝖙𝖑𝖊, ITC-049

Typography design for this volume was inspired by the elegant details of Continent journal. Thus the text is set in Frutiger LT Std, a variant of the Frutiger typeface often used on pharmaceutical labels due to its legibility. Adrian Frutiger's life was filled with tragedy, losing his first wife in childbirth and the two daughters of his second marriage to Selbstmord. His sans-serif typeface is used in Amtrak branding. Titles are set in Memphis Light.

Cover design was inspired by the xerography of Deepskin Conceptual Mindmusic cassette releases of Clinton Williams' experimental electronics act Omit.

Both of these touchstones were curated by Maure Coise to enhance the physical characterization of these volumes and their congruency with the mission of the text.

Designed by John Trefry for 𝕴𝖓𝖘𝖎𝖉𝖊 𝖙𝖍𝖊 𝕮𝖆𝖘𝖙𝖑𝖊

ISBN-13: 979-8-9870838-7-1

Structuring Information is a text in the expanded field of literature.
Visit www.insidethecastle.org for more.
𝕴𝖓𝖘𝖎𝖉𝖊 𝖙𝖍𝖊 𝕮𝖆𝖘𝖙𝖑𝖊 is located in Lawrence, Kansas

Structuring Information:
Internet Energy Intensity and Efficiencies Volume 3

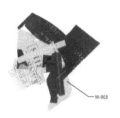

Maure Coise

also in **Internet Energy Intensity and Efficiencies**
Volume 1: Cultural Object Ontologies by Maure Coise, 2019
Volume 2: Ontologies of Environmental Collapse by Nuala Loges, 2021
Volume 3: Structuring Information by Maure Coise, 2023

Winter 2023, Lawrence, Kansas, 110pp., $13

Structuring Information

```
CREATE DATABASE "StructuringInformation";
GO
```

```
USE "StructuringInformation";
GO
```

```sql
CREATE TABLE dbo.BronwenAndNualaMoveIntoTheirNewApartmentInNewHav-
en
(
TheFatherOfBronwenAssistsInTheMove varchar(400) NOT NULL PRIMARY KEY,
ThereAreManyNeighborhoodsTheyWouldHavePreferredToMoveInto varchar(500)
NOT NULL
);

INSERT INTO dbo. BronwenAndNualaMoveIntoTheirNewApartmentInNewHaven
(TheFatherOfBronwenAssistsInTheMove, ThereAreManyNeighborhoodsThey-
WouldHavePreferredToMoveInto)
VALUES ('Bronwen's father enjoyed the importance of his position. He'd op-
posed them moving so far away and in together. So much so he hadn't spoken
much to anyone for five months prior. It was in his house that Bronwen and
Nuala had sex. Bronwen's father would light a cigar and listen. In the night
of the move he got a hotel room. And he left in the morning.', 'Bronwen and
Nuala found that they could get everything they needed at the farmer's market.
They walked down their street, taking in the spring-like aroma of the August air.
Many of the apartments on the street were basement apartments, like Nuala
lived in as a child. There was a park nearby, where they picnicked. Nuala had
never had a sandwich with mustard,mayonnaise and pickles. Nuala had been to
that very park before. He visited New Haven years ago and became a vegetari-
an.')
;
```

```sql
CREATE TABLE dbo.NualaHasAJobAtTheArchdiocese
(
HerSupervisorMightHaveBeenAnAcademicInAnotherTown varchar(400) NOT NULL
PRIMARY KEY,
NualaSaysSheWasInterestedInTheConceptualAchievementsOfChristianity
varchar(220) NOT NULL,
SheLikesThatHerSupervisorCallsTheHigherUpsTheDarkOnes varchar(300) NOT NULL
);


INSERT INTO dbo. BronwenHasAJobAtTheArchdiocese
(HerSupervisorMightHaveBeenAnAcademicInAnotherTown, NualaSaysSheWasInter-
estedInTheConceptualAchievementsOfChristianity, SheLikesThatHisSupervisorCalls-
TheHigherUpsTheDarkOnes)
VALUES
('Boguslaw showed Nuala her tasks, to digitalize the Fathers' correspondences and
build a system to search the archive. Boguslaw taught Nuala an unusual metadata
scheme. It involved inputting contradictory values. A letter from Boguslaw to Paul
was to be cataloged as also a letter from Paul to Boguslaw.', 'Boguslaw and Nuala
sat in the clean office, facing each other. Boguslaw tried to force some intimacy.
"We are all curious why such a young man is interested in this work... I've arranged
some private meetings with one of the Fathers for you."', 'Nuala tried to avoid
saying something overly psychological.'),
('"When I first started here," Boguslaw continued, "it was daylight savings time
and I had forgotten. So, I arrived late on my first day."', 'On some occasions, at par-
ties, Nuala sometimes, for no apparent reason, dropped her glass. When her drink
spilled, he'd make an effort to clean it without anyone noticing', '"I think," Bogu-
slaw continued, absentmindedly, "it is a good idea for you to come to a concert
here. Not in this building, but in the other building, where are public services are.'),
('Nuala decided against bringing Bronwen to this concert. Throughout the day he
thought about their previous two nights alone together. Invigorated. On her way
to the office he had seen construction workers digging a hole, for no discernible
reason.', 'Near the famous gardens in Padua, Nuala once heard the chorus of the
cathedral sing a complex harmony. It evoked a deep feeling in Nuala that she never
forgot, but he had no identifying details of the music.', 'Memories embed in mem-
ories. Nuala associated that moment with her father telling him that if she kept her
hands in her pockets people would think she was masturbating. When she brought
home fleas, her father insisted on finding out exactly where she got them.')
;
```

```
CREATE TABLE dbo.NualaAtTheConcert
(SheNoticesManyFacesHeHadSeenEarlier varchar(500) NOT NULL PRIMARY KEY,
SheDoesNotWantToBeSeen varchar(700) NOT NULL
);


INSERT INTO dbo. NualaAtTheConcert (SheNoticesManyFacesHeHadSeenEarlier,
SheDoesNotWantToBeSeen)
VALUES
('Foldout chairs were assembled in rows circling a grand piano. Boguslaw
approached as Nuala sat. "Ah, did you pay?" "Oh, no." Nuala fumbled. "How
much?" "$10." Boguslaw collected the fee and walked away. Two elderly
women having a conversation sat down on either side of Nuala. Uncontrollably,
Nuala became wet. It only subsided when the pianist began. Nuala tried to pay
attention to the music.', 'Transfixed by the simple resolution of E#, E, A, Bb, with
a wheezing vibrato, Nuala remembered being anxious to get somewhere, and
having to take the bus. So anxious, all he had was a five dollar bill, so she put
it in and will never forget the look of horror and disgust the bus driver gave.
She was offended at the gesture of irresponsibility, to flaunt how little $2.50
meant to him.Through her left shoulder, she felt a sharp pain that opened up
her wrists, and stung deep in the left side of her face. For the pianist, the pieces
reminded of rolling grasslands, with a beet red color. A jagged line would have
served as notation. In only a few bars, she expressed what she did not know')
;
```

```sql
CREATE TABLE dbo.BronwenCrying
(
NualaAsksWhatIsWrong varchar(400) NOT NULL PRIMARY KEY,
HerQuestionImpliesAnotherQuestionAreYouUnhappyHere varchar(80) NOT NULL,
NualaTriesToDoNothing varchar(250) NOT NULL,
SheCannotControlTheAtmosphere varchar(225) NOT NULL
);


INSERT INTO dbo.BronwenCrying (NualaAsksWhatIsWrong, HerQuestionImpliesAn-
otherQuestionAreYouUnhappyHere, NualaTriesToDoNothing, SheCannotControlThe-
Atmosphere)
VALUES
('She felt like she couldn't breathe properly. She thought she was the cause of her
bodily contortions. Narcissistic hate paralleled her grief. She made dinner and pout-
ed when she didn't respond to her call, "time to eat." She experienced this many
times. She didn't like New Haven. She went to the bedroom. She wanted to throw
a book at him.', 'Both Bronwen and she was raised atheist, but each had a Catholic
and a Protestant raised parent, a Catholic dad and mom, respectively.', 'Bronwen
came in. "I'm ok now."', 'Nuala almost spoke about the concert. Then a small box
on a bookshelf flew off, as if thrown, and landed on the floor. Upstairs their circus
freak neighbour with the pillbox hat was fucking loudly.'),
('Bronwen and Nuala wanted to stay together. Feel into their little selves and
connect their hearts and say whetever came to their mind. They never saw their
yearlong lease as a commitment. They draped vintage Sax 5th ave silks on every-
thing.', '"Do you want to watch something?"', 'They never thought of going out,
but watched movies on their emac with its butterfly sticker.', 'They spoke of a used
furniture store where they wanted to buy a round low level tabel with engraved
ring pass knots. A homeless man, also from Florida, would carry it for them on his
head, but accidentally break a hole through the center.')
;
```

```
CREATE TABLE dbo.IThinkGodIsAnEfficiency
(SheSaidTalkingToPaul varchar(900) NOT NULL PRIMARY KEY
REFERENCES NualaAtTheConcert (SheNoticesManyFaceSheHadSeenEarlier),
TheyWereTalkingAboutAdam varchar(540) NOT NULL
);


INSERT INTO dbo.IThinkGodIsAnEfficiency (SheSaidTalkingToPaul, TheyWere-
TalkingAboutAdam)
VALUES
```

('"The origin of creation contains the seed of evil. Salvation comes with the apocalypse and has already come, with the Messiah. They converge in the fire Christ brought." "That is the origin?" "You are thinking too mechanically." He gave Nuala an exercise to think about prime numbers, to ask himself, on buses, for example, to consider if the numbers displayed were prime. And also, advised to practice counting up 1, 2, 4, 8, up to 100 and back. They ended their session with ten minutes of silent prayer. Nuala thought Paul could access his consciousness. He didn't want him to think he was paranoid. Something circulated between them for those ten minutes. Paul would have said it was grace bestowed on them by invisible beings. If such beings could be summoned, Nuala thought, why weren't they more frequently?', 'The Church was made of brick and the grounds were concrete. The concrete transformed to a carpet of brick, stretching out and returning to concrete. The Church itself turned into a concrete slab. Nuala had a horrible feeling that something would burst up from below, grab her and drive him mad. She had a grilled cheese accidentally made with banana bread.'),

('8 hours on a computer was a long time for Nuala. She had to stare at a document for several minutes before grasping anything of its content.', 'She worked alone in the office that day. There was a cart of materials waiting for him to process. She worked slowly, checking the Library of Congress website to verify the standards and the RDA toolkit for best practices. He opened the software that looked like a spreadsheet. Rows were fields to encode, author, date, and other information to signify subject. She linked the description to an authority record in the database. In the '655' field, he noted the Biblical allusions. She mostly left those incomplete. Otherwise, she'd created 13 records in his first 2 days. It was a slow process, to familiarize with the style of the Fathers' correspondences. And she hadn't even started transcribing. And she set aside the search engines.'),

('Although, it has fallen out of fashion, she planned to design a Topic Map for search.', 'It was better to work for the Church than have to do metadata design for sales auctions. The texts, although bureaucratic, had piercing clarity. As she was working he noticed that someone outside the window was watching him.

She didn't have time to discern its features before it leaned in and began crawling toward Nuala on all fours. "Stop." Nuala cried. The figure disappeared. She rushed to the window. She tried to recreate the image of the figure in her memory, a shadow, and did the eyes reflect some light? She felt concerned for the equipment in the room, as if it were a potential break in.'),

('The next letter read: Dear Joseph Haigh, I am organizing a team to appraise electricity usage. Here in New Haven, we are responsible for all educational programs in the Eastern United States. A review board of academics help us with proposals, as well as grants. The question concerning amplification, electricity use in music and spoken programs will be forwarded to both teams.... Nuala looked for another page. She couldn't find any letters from Mr. Haigh. She thought the topic might be theology. But, she typed music, electricity, and education. Linking the record to all correspondences dealing with public utilities for the building. She noticed a breeze again. She got up and peered out the window. It was a crisp August day, brown rooftops and an acidic smell. She tried to think of Biblical allusions. She tried to think of the opposite of music. Unamplified music?', 'She typed the symbol, ‡. She was using a lot of electricity. The anti-field was not meant to negate the key topics. Paul had explicitly rejected any thought of via negativa mysticism.')

;

```
CREATE TABLE dbo.TheConcertHasPedagogicalValue
(
NualaListenedWithoutContext varchar(70) NOT NULL PRIMARY KEY
REFERENCES NualaAtTheConcert (SheNoticesManyFacesSheHadSeenEarlier),
IThinkGodIsAnEfficiency (SheSaidTalkingToPaul),
SheDidn'tKnowTheNamesOfThePieces varchar(45) NOT NULL,
ThereWasAmplificationAndSheDidFindItDistracting varchar(85) NOT NULL
);


INSERT INTO dbo.TheConcertHasPedagogicalValue (NualaListenedWithoutCon-
text, SheDidn'tKnowTheNamesOfThePieces, ThereWasAmplificationAndSheDid-
FindItDistracting)
VALUES
('Nuala failed in her love for Bronwen. Change was impossible.', 'Nuala
attended only to her right side.', 'In 2008, Bronwen and Nuala wanted to have
children. This wasn't fulfilled.')
;
```

```
CREATE FUNCTION dbo.BronwenDoesNotLikeToGoOut (@BronwenGoesToTheGem-
Store mural)
RETURNS mural
AS
BEGIN
DECLARE @mural =
(SELECT TheConcertHasPedagogicalValue
FROM NualaAtTheConcert et
JOIN TheConcertHasPedagogicalValue e
ON et. SheNoticesManyFacesHeHadSeenEarlier = e.BronwenGoesToTheGemStore
WHERE TheConcertHasPedagogicalValue = @TheConcertHasPedagogicalValue);
DECLARE @SheCutHerselfOffFromEveryoneSheKnewBefore mural = CHRIST(@
mural,
@BronwenGoesToTheGemStore);
RETURN @SheCutHerselfOffFromEveryoneSheKnewBefore;
END
GO
```

```
CREATE TABLE dbo.ItWasNotThatBronwenWantedAServanttButThatWasAllNual-
aCouldProvide
(
SheCutHerselfOffFromEveryoneSheKnewBefore varchar(45) NOT NULL PRIMARY
KEY,
REFERENCES NualaAtTheConcert(HeNoticesManyFacesSheHadSeenEarlier),
IThinkGodIsAnEfficiency (SheSaidTalkingToPaul), TheConcertHasPedagogicalVal-
ue(NualaListenedWithoutContext),
OnceSheSawChristWave varchar(40) NOT NULL,
SheAlwaysHadToRemindNualaToRubHerClitorisClockwiseAndWithASteady-
Rhythm varchar(150) NOT NULL
);

INSERT INTO dbo. ItWasNotThatBronwenWantedAServanttButThatWasAllNual-
aCouldProvide (SheCutHerselfOffFromEveryoneSheKnewBefore, OnceSheSaw-
ChristWave, SheAlwaysHadToRemindNualaToRubHerClitorisClockwiseAndWith-
ASteadyRhythm)
VALUES
('Nuala was always silent', 'She took birth control.', 'After a few months in New
Haven she stopped.'),
('They went to a museum with her friend Yulia.', 'The museum was in Bronwen
and Nuala's neighbourhood. The only building with modernist architecture, glass
and steel hexagons.', 'Bronwen had a clear image of playing with her children in
the garden.')
;
```

```
CREATE TABLE dbo.NualaThinksSheIsBetterThanEveryone
(WhatIsHerHumor varchar(20) NOT NULL PRIMARY KEY,
Bilious varchar(35) NOT NULL
);

INSERT INTO dbo.NualaThinksSeIsBetterThanEveryone (WhatIsHerHumor, Bilious)
VALUES
('"His temperament?", Yulia asked. ', 'She is arrogant and authoritarian. She only
wanted to be a preacher or whatever to appease her mother. It was a downward
aspiration. She didn't live in this world.')
;
```

```
CREATE MASTER KEY
ENCRYPTION BY PASSWORD = 'ReallyNualaWhatAreYouRunningFrom';
CREATE CERTIFICATE End WITH SUBJECT = 'Not seeing anyone... why are you
hiding?', EXPIRY_Date = '2028-06-01';
CREATE SYMMETRIC KEY ReallyNualaWhatAreYouRunningFromSymmetricKey
WITH ALGORITHM = AES_128
ENCRYPTION BY CERTIFICATE End;
OPEN SYMMETRIC KEY ReallyNualaWhatAreYouRunningFromSymmetricKey
DECRYPTION BY CERTIFICATE End;
UPDATE dbo.NualaThinksSheIsBetterThanEveryone
SET EncWhatIsHerHumor = EncryptByKey (Key_GUID (N'ReallyNualaWhatAr-
eYouRunningFromSymmetricKey'), Bilious,pm);
CLOSE SYMMETRIC KEY ReallyNualaWhatAreYouRunningFromSymmetricKey;
DROP SYMMETRIC KEY ReallyNualaWhatAreYouRunningFromSymmetricKey;
DROP CERTIFICATE End;
DROP MASTER KEY
;
```

```sql
CREATE TABLE dbo.AsYouNoticeLikesAndDislikesWhatRemainsUnshakenIsCon-
science
(IAmSoFragmented varchar(80) NOT NULL PRIMARY KEY,
HaveYouTriedJogging varchar(150) NOT NULL
);

INSERT INTO dbo. AsYouNoticeLikesAndDislikesWhatRemainsUnshakenIsConscience
(IAmSoFragmented, HaveYouTriedJogging)
VALUES ('"Have you read my poems?"', '"Yes. I couldn't get anything from them.
They seemed like a thesaurus wrote them. You need to focus on loosening up.
Observe your facial expressions."'),
('"That would only increase my nervousness."', '"Have you tried? If so, that is an
opportunity to observe what is most likely laziness."'),
('"I don't like to ask myself, at the end of the day, what I did right or wrong."',
'"You philosophize to the point of worthlessness. You need to learn social and
physiological grace."')
;
```

```
CREATE TABLE dbo.ReadingOvid
(
HeIsInterestingBecauseHeDoesNotWorkWithDistinctCategoriesOfPastoralOr-
TragicAsMuchAsHisStartingPointIsTheIdyll varchar(40) NOT NULL PRIMARY
KEY,
IsItLyricism varchar(20) NOT NULL,
TakeThePolyphemusAndGalateaStory varchar(20) NOT NULL
);


INSERT INTO dbo.ReadingOvid
(HeIsInterestingBecauseHeDoesNotWorkWithDistinctCategoriesOfPastoralOr-
TragicAsMuchAsHisStartingPointIsTheIdyll, IsItLyricism, TakeThePolyphemu-
sAndGalateaStory)
VALUES
```

('Ovid doesn't make the lyricism the ground for an epic mode. Polyphemus courts Galatea by listing life's pleasures, by describing the scenery. This unifies pastoral and tragic. The power play between them is tragic, initiatory. "But, it is such a short story." "It doesn't matter, it is a recursive fragment." "Are you saying something about the form?" "No, I am saying the love of Polyphemus is the landscape. His invitation." "To what?" "To the lyrical form. Like you said, to the extent that it leads to low cortical arousal." "I think," said Nuala, "Ovid had a inner sense creating a separation, I mean, creating a boundary is either more than itself or less. Ovid's invitation, or Polyphemus's, has the goal of carrying you beyond empirical limits, into a shared reality, seeking what it is to be symbolized." "And Polyphemus unquestionably fails."', '"I think the site of art, the mind, is just conditions of neural synaptic states. The lyricism, ok, the pastoral or tragic modes assume some regulatory functions of the creative act. And Ovid is very true to the event, because of how he handles differences in modes. And also, mixing traditional myths with his own. But, I mean, how the modes or priors shape the conceptualization of the lyricism, the feeling or affect. Like a painter has to start somewhere, but the arbitrary starting line constrains every further line."', 'Bronwen dreamt she was crossing the border. There were no signs. She felt like she knew where she was. And that it had taken a long time to get here. She looked at a map and the highway she was on glowed blue. She remembered someone was waiting for her. When they would appear, everything would make sense.'),

('Nuala had halfheartedly choked her. Bronwen took some sleeping pills. Nuala increasingly disapproved of everything Bronwen did.', 'In a prayer, she asked for a personification of everything he hated. She appeared, winged.', 'Bronwen didn't meditate. She worked by intuition. She wasn't interested

in axe murderers. She read the classics for the scenery. She loved the strange, fantastic elements, especially when they were invisible, only glimpsed.')
;

```sql
CREATE TABLE dbo.AnythingNualaDidWouldGoWrong
(SheWasPerscuted varchar(35) NOT NULL PRIMARY KEY,
WasSheLookingForPunishment varchar(40) NOT NULL
);

INSERT INTO dbo.AnythingNualaDidWouldGoWrong (SheWasPerscuted, WasSheLookingForPunishment)
VALUES
```
('She was constantly the object of scorn, 'She looked for escape from social tensions in any way, except she didn't drink. And because of this she had no way of meeting people.'),
('Her family didn't have a computer until 2003. She had a hard time finding an interest, until she found Amazon.com and she loved looking for books and music, following the recommendations.', 'Bronwen has computers all her life. Her father worked with them. Passion for directing energy to the computer, bound to persecution, anticipated rejection.'),
('Nuala's family computer was in her bedroom. Her father would "knock, knock, I need to use the computer." Now she got ominous emails. Berating her from taking money from her mother. She covered her rent. Long ago, she thought her parents asked her which of them she preferred. "I play with dad in the daytime, mom at night. There is more time in the daytime, so dad." He worked nightshifts. Ingrained, today I did A, B, C. Saying A, B, C in French came with toasted baguette slices.', ' Their house was always musty. Everything was from the 1970s. Everything her father said he repeated. His words were built into Nuala's structure of thinking. Her childhood neighbourhood was also, built in. The personality of every house, the glass orb on the pillar, next to the 'beware of dog' sign.')
;

```
CREATE TABLE dbo.NualaLookedForStillness
(
LookingIntoTheCorrelationsOfCorrespondenceAndTheConceptualOriginsInTheBible
varchar(75) NOT NULL PRIMARY KEY,
InTheTriadicMediationOfConnectionAndConditions varchar(80) NOT NULL,
TranslatingInitiatesAnInterpretation varchar(150) NOT NULL,
TheCategoryOfRelationAscendsAndDescendsAndCondescends varchar(25) NOT
NULL
);
```

INSERT INTO dbo.NualaLookedForStillness (LookingIntoTheCorrelationsOfCorre-
spondenceAndTheConceptualOriginsInTheBible, InTheTriadicMediationOfConnec-
tionAndConditions, TranslatingInitiatesAnInterpretation, TheCategoryOfRelationA-
scendsAndDescendsAndCondescends)
VALUES
('"When Paul writes, in Romans 9, God gives the reed, is that an imperative or a
declarative?"', ' Paul replied, "The Father's power prefigures the love of the son.
Paul treats the body in terms of knowledge. When word becomes flesh, it is much
like, when you are asked questions you cannot possibly answer, but that open
up the space, a potential. Envisioning a likeness, forming an image. It is internal-
ized. You respond always to your name. It is like the place you stand."', '"I don't
understand the metaphor." Nuala replied. "Touch brings us closer to abolishing
predicates how?"', '"Your speech is confused." Paul replied. He thinks, this is why
she rejects language, to organize the world in her image."'),
('"I'm looking for the words"', 'The Armenian, Syrian, Egyptian, and Ethiopian
Churches maintain the position that God has One Nature incarnated as the word.
This stems from debates on the relation of Father and Son. In what sense did
the human parents of the Son birth God? The Oneness of God is not an ordinal
number, nor is it dialectical. For miaphysite Churches, it is a hypostatic unity.', 'The
apprehension of human and divine difference in identity is a determination of pure
knowledge. It repeats, as a recursive reciprocation of the past in every relation, the
function determining knowledge. The thought of the origin certifies the verifica-
tion of ensured separation. The prerogative of an impossible task, determining the
generation of the determinable, as the conditions of the origin, unconscious, formal,
divisibility, in the continuity of the act of the determinable determined determining
the determination of the determinable determining according to an operation prior
to affirmation or negation, constituting an integration of the known, construct-
ing knowledge. The logical classification of validation programs determination,
synthesizing conditioned concepts a priori, validating determination as generating
consciousness, expanding categories, pure knowledge encompasses the determin-

able determining the determined as a determination, appraising the transformations of categorical distinctions. The pure is undetermined determinateness, the determinability of determination.', 'The pure thought, the circle of unconditioned conditioning, is not just a classificatory method, explaining the limits of thinking, but delimits the discrimination of validation as intensive magnitudes, sense data differentiation and integration in laws. A mathematical differential transfers undercurrent symbolization as temporal organization. Ignoring the asymptotic aspects of placing a future, desire binds histories in recognition and reciprocation.')

;

```
CREATE TABLE dbo.RejectingBronwen
(
AdoptionOfCertainPitchModulationsInVoice varchar(275) NOT NULL PRIMARY KEY
SeeingHerAsMoreDomineeringAndWantingMoreOfHerAttention varchar(140) NOT
NULL
);
```

INSERT INTO dbo. RejectingBronwen (AdoptionOfCertainPitchModulationsInVoice,
SeeingHerAsMoreDomineeringAndWantingMoreOfHerAttention)
VALUES
('Bronwen became very interested in muscle tissue therapy. Muscle cells form fibers
to contract, chemistry transforms mechanics, see spindle shaped smooth muscles
differ from specialized fibers hooked to vessels pumping blood, conducting electrical
impulses. Between muscles, fascia or tendons, structure connective tissue, fibrations,
structure-connecting nerves with synaptic gap cleft, transmitting electrical impulses.
Creation of muscle, processing proteins, parallel adipose, or fat, like cholesterol
nourishing glands, secreting, for example, acetylcholine. ', 'Bronwen visualized her
hips. Bringing attention to her knees, muscles around the knees, attaching to bones
through ligaments to periosteum, whose calcium levels correlate to hormones, deep
in the bone, red and yellow marrow, like cranial nerves, in the anterior frontal lobes
opening to the hypothalamus, storing memory of cell mitosis. Occurring through
zygotes.'),
('Prior to the first breath, in embryogenesis, there is a capacity for stereognosis. The
spinal column opens to the fourth ventricle, the inferior horn of the lateral ventricle,
choroid plexuses, secreting cerebrospinal fluid. Enhancing the ability to send electri-
cal signals. Using those impulses to direct to the heart, protein, zinc, and mercury.',
'Nuala started masturbating at age 13. She stopped at 16. And started back up at
20. She stopped when he was making love to Bronwen. Her addiction damaged her.
Bronwen studied the porosities between cells, the back and forth of oxygen, carbon
dioxide, and potassium ions; the dilation of channels, across all tissues, secreting
adrenocortical hormones, with enzymes respective to each tissue.
'),
('She did not consider the extent to which he wanted to control others, now, espe-
cially. His breath wasn't going down to his diaphragm.', ' The pineal gland governs
the pacemaker, stabilizing tissues through red blood cells. A metabolic dynamic like
a vector, descending through the vagus nerve, cardiac activity increases hydrochloric
acid secretion, ascending sympathetic to parasympathetic. The hypothalamus sends
messages to intercostal muscles to contract and fill lungs with carbon dioxide. This
is not a mechanism. The upper lobes of the lung welcome ozone, the oxidizing
agent in the decaying body. Bronwen and Nuala were fatigued, from the sciatic

nerve to the colon. Ptyalin in the saliva aids electrolyte balance. Food passes down to the stomach and fundus releases and gastric mucus is secreted. Gastrin, a hormone stimulates pepsin to digest proteins. Passing through small intestines, emulsification, the pyloric valve opens, bile alkalizes, chyle is absorbed, nutrients, vitamins, minerals, digested. Amino acids store and carry memories. Molecules circulating, producing peptides, chaining together into pathways in nuclear membranes, forming RNA and DNA, producing content of cytoplasm.'),

;

```sql
CREATE TABLE dbo.SomethingWasLostInTheGut
 (
CuminAndFennelAndCilantroAndTurmericAndSaffronAndCardamom varchar(40)
NOT NULL PRIMARY KEY
TheyDreamtOfTheirGarden varchar(45) NOT NULL,
TheyWantedToGrowTheirOwnFoodToHelpTheirDigestion varchar(45) NOT NULL
);

INSERT INTO dbo. SomethingWasLostInTheGut (CuminAndFennelAndCilan-
troAndTurmericAndSaffronAndCardamom, TheyDreamtOfTheirGarden, TheyWanted-
ToGrowTheirOwnFoodToHelpTheirDigestion)
VALUES
('They dreamt of tilling the Earth, acquiring manure and straw, growing burdock
and clover. ', 'They drew pictures of paths in their dream garden, imagined its pH
levels, watering brings a chemical solvent to safely grow leafy greens surrounded by
berry bushes', 'They were bloated '),
('Bronwen's study of metabolism, cell permeability, was critical. Cilantro, but also
mint, and basil, surrounded by raspberry. Mugwort is an emmenagogue, warm-
ing the lower abdomen, clearing out the nerve channels, if you want to act with
direction, relieving tension, unpleasant physical manifestation.', 'Nuala only wanted
excitement. His ego was a reactive stabilizing force. Neurosis decreased possibility
for action. Passivity, he had a desire to return to his mother's pregnancy, in-animacy.
To study germ cells, Protista conjugations. He didn't like the metaphor of informa-
tion, code. Organization collects many origins. There is no gene-environment binary.
The nucleus of a zygote doesn't merely print instructions on cytoplasm. But, how
do you explain the relation of inheritance but through the analytic of genotype and
ontogeny and then, phenotype and phylogeny? Adapting and differentiating hor-
mones, Nuala wanted to believe in a priori plan to chromosomes, raising her arm,
isolating sensations, ingesting, she needed lubrication, to have a sensation in her
cranial cavity, concentration, moving to the bronchi, trachea.', ' Heating and cooling
herbs can be used excessively. Ginseng and angelica are good for regeneration.')
;
```

```sql
CREATE TABLE dbo.TheGarden
(
Comfrey varchar(30) NOT NULL PRIMARY KEY,
BurdockAndYellowDock varchar(25) NOT NULL
);
```

```sql
INSERT INTO dbo.TheGarden (Comfrey, BurdockAndYellowDock)
VALUES ('They were unaffected by seasonal change', 'When Nuala bought
Bronwen a beer at the corner store, she paid the two dollar service fee on the
ATM to pay for the beer in cash'),
('In Florida, they used to be driven around in cars so much', 'There was no value
in higher education after the housing collapse. The bank bailouts consolidated
what had convinced their own parents to break from sedentary living only to
collapse under the weight of domestic appliances and mortgages'),
('They look at their black neighbors from above. They were not extras', 'They
both digested peaches very well')
('Both had negative experiences with doctors', 'Spending all of their time
together, they never sought friends, yet they had little to show for all their
self-healing, fighting often, and often having indigestion')
('Nuala was physically light, les heat, immobile in mood. Bony, delicate, easily
excited mentally, but lazy, with dry hair and poor circulation', 'Bronwen was
larger in frame, with whiter skin and hormonal imbalances. Good pepsin and
hemoglobin, white lymphs, strong myelin sheaths around her nerve axons,
strong mucosal lining and synovial fluid'),
;
```

```sql
CREATE TABLE dbo.ReproductiveTissueDisorder
(
NualaShouldHaveCheckedHerPulseMore varchar(40) NOT NULL PRIMARY KEY,
TheTransitOfRedBloodCellProductionFromLiverAndSpleenToBoneMarrowWasTrau-
maticInHerBirth varchar(20) NOT NULL,
);


INSERT INTO dbo.ReproductiveTissueDisorder
(NualaShouldHaveCheckedHerPulseMore, TheTransitOfRedBloodCellProduction-
FromLiverAndSpleenToBoneMarrowWasTraumaticInHerBirth)
VALUES
('It didn't seem ischmatic', 'Senses, giving rise to intuitions, give rise to the intuit-
ed'),
('She couldn't pinpoint her anxiety', 'To digest well, to secrete enzymes, she looked
to fenugreek, turmeric, cumin, fennel'),
('The lifecycle of cells, anabolism, when one takes over another, is this mind?', 'Cells
pass into each other, expanding and contracting')
;
```

```sql
CREATE TABLE dbo.Metamorphoses
(OvidDissolvesBoundaries varchar(35) NOT NULL PRIMARY KEY,
PresentingAWayOfLivingAndBeingInTheWorld varchar(40) NOT NULL
);

INSERT INTO dbo.Metamorphoses (OvidDissolvesBoundaries, PresentingAWay-
OfLivingAndBeingInTheWorld)
VALUES
('While Nuala had slow anabolism, she had fast catabolism', 'Like a vessel
kindling energy into a liquid'),
('Phases of metabolism, sped up, more or less', 'Different enzymes form tissue,
gastric mucus to liver enzymes, catalyzed by chewing, breaking down proteins
with peptides'),
('Peptide chains correspond to neurotransmitters', 'Nuala overate fruits'),
('Ovid sometimes speeds up metamorphoses, saying "he noticed his feathers
change color before ever noting that "he suddenly had feathers"', 'Paul wanted
non-Jews to become Christians. In Acts 17, he says Christ is the One king, all
are unified because the end and the resurrection has been ordained')
;
```

```sql
CREATE TABLE dbo.NualaFeltHerHumanFormReturn
(
InTheGardenNualaCarriedHematiteWithin varchar(75) NOT NULL PRIMARY KEY,
BuildingMagnetism varchar(80) NOT NULL,
SheLooksAtHerBackAsItTurnsToStone varchar(150) NOT NULL,
Straightening varchar(25) NOT NULL
);


INSERT INTO dbo.NualaFeltHerHumanFormReturn (InTheGardenNualaCarriedHema-
titeWithin, BuildingMagnetism, SheLooksAtHerBackAsItTurnsToStone, Straightening)
VALUES
('Her frame dissolves', 'Her head bubbles upward like a boil on a hematite', 'Glisten-
ing, rough cut, she becomes a stone pillar', 'Very slowly'),
('She reaches out as if shooting a bow and arrow', 'Twisting what were once arms',
'In a half circle, front and back', 'Her heart no longer itched, sensitive to any touch.
Stomach and intestines and gut were gone'),
('Her right hip no longer jut out', 'Now, beginning to exert some semblance of a
will, everything in her vision vibrated, each particle in each molecule seemed to
show itself', 'Turning into hematite', 'The sun beat down on the mass of hematite'),
('To accept the repose offered by some future vision of a fruitful place that the
stone was a part of', 'Some deer passed by', 'Some campers set up a tent', 'They
had come to build a fence to keep the deer out'),
('Nuala felt nothing and noticed them coming and going', 'Day to night, Nuala was
hematite', 'Still. Feeling particles of dirt', 'The energy built up disappeared')
;
```

```
CREATE TABLE dbo.Millet
(
CellWallsPassUndigested varchar(275) NOT NULL PRIMARY KEY
OneSeed varchar(140) NOT NULL
);


INSERT INTO dbo.Millet (CellWallsPassUndigested, OneSeed)
VALUES
('Millet has an endosperm, bran, and a germ', 'It's outer layers have vitamin B'),
('The broccoli supplied the vitamin A', 'She felt nerve damage in her pulse, a
serpentine wavering'),
('To avoid overexposure to the Internet, she needed a teleology relating life and
it's mechanical maintenance', 'Touch through an interface differed from touch-
ing Bronwen, but laughing at a joke online was not laughing alone')
;
```

```
CREATE TABLE dbo.Polysemy
(
ATagLikeLightOrGreen varchar(40) NOT NULL PRIMARY KEY
WithMultipleMeanings varchar(45) NOT NULL,
WithSharedSemanticRelations varchar(45) NOT NULL
);
```

INSERT INTO dbo.Polysemy (ATagLikeLightOrGreen, WithMultipleMeanings, With-
SharedSemanticRelations)
VALUES
('A critical problem for search function that do more than mark texts and arrange
hierarchies of marks, but reference in relation to use; that, more than map syntag-
matic relations, position levels of metaphor. What is a machine-readable informa-
tion retrieval that integrates the determination of indirect intention? To formalize
words' meanings, as a function of syntactic combination, for example, anaphora,
carrying references, through a chain, to an indirect reference, one might hardcode
a modal logic, degrees of possibility; coding parameters for type shifting and noun
phrase parsing. The problem is that there are sometimes no clear patterns for
metaphoric language. By building a lexicon, in XML, of morphological, phonetic,
and semantic units, the grammatical differences of polysemous keywords might
be accounted for through pairing words with contradictory words, more or less
complementary or converse, although no taxonomy could ever completely contain
the variability of pairing', ' A tag like good could be analyzed through co-occurrence
of uses as dialectically relating to particular contradictory words (as opposed to an-
alyzing the expectation of sense according to prior words in paragraph). To analyze
relations of contradiction, the markedness of markers classified as lexical relations,
links between nodes, typed (as a sense), according to the conditions of revisability.
Building a lexicon through negation, the value of a function could be modeled, like
a thesaurus, to process meaningfulness of information, not as a type of entailment,
but the limits of entailment, through acceptable grouping of uses of contradictory
pairing. This intensional basis for a selective model of the database structured
semantic memory. The building blocks of type, the token, are not based on similar-
ity, but the differences in sharing properties. Intensional contradictions, rather than
semantic equivalences, determine the decision of a position on a register, instanti-
ating a variant', '"I want the green", what is the sense of this "green"? Underlying
contradictory pairing might provide an answer deeper than any context. Forcing
the problem of function into a taxonomic problem, a nominal type-token structure
might bypass syntax, leveraging difference for inclusive reference. A higher order
lexicon need also be constructed to account for head phrase structure grammar
analytic of verb relations. In Mandarin, verbs are often used like nouns and also

as ways of measuring, modifiers that are more or less adjectival, and more or less tensed, like piecing-rope or lengthening-rope. Further Mandarins presents complexity in word segmentation itself, we might parse "people talk a lot" to mean, metaphorically, "there are a lot of people present"')
;

```
CREATE TABLE dbo.NualaWantedFreePlay
(
SheWasDevotedWIthoutCourtesy varchar(30) NOT NULL PRIMARY KEY,
ClingingCodependenceWasAConstraint varchar(25) NOT NULL
);

INSERT INTO dbo.NualaWantedFreePlay (SheWasDevotedWIthoutCourtesy, Cling-
ingCodependenceWasAConstraint)
VALUES ('Bronwen was flung in too quickly. Taking on Nuala's parents problems', '
From the beginning, there was competition'),
('She didn't want her children to have them as grandparents.  Although her parents
were also coming from a long line of Midwestern laborers', 'Nuala won her from
her friend group. She expected everything from her, but couldn't meet her. '),
('Their parents were more austere, and more hedonistic', 'Nuala's heart clenched,
his left side tensed. Gretchen was his surrogate conscience. Once when she was
eight years old he was visited by a devilish figure in her bedroom, while she lay in
bed and her parents watched TV. The figure had glowing eyes and horns. Standing
at the door')
;
```

```sql
CREATE TABLE dbo.WhatAreYouGettingOutOfChristianity
(
HerFatherAskedOnThePhoneExpectingPerfectionToComeFromRoutine
varchar(40) NOT NULL PRIMARY KEY,
DoYouBelieveInSinNow varchar(20) NOT NULL,
);

INSERT INTO dbo.WhatAreYouGettingOutOfChristianity
(HerFatherAskedOnThePhoneExpectingPerfectionToComeFromRoutine, DoYouBelieveInSinNow)
VALUES
('Nuala thought her mother had gone to Catholic school, but it was just Sunday
school. And she stopped going after her first communion', 'Nuala never liked
the pressure of choosing what to do. She had to choose something that every-
one would like'),
('She believed what she learned from Paul differed from what her parents had
learned in Church', 'She lost her spark. She tried to commit himself, harder to a
mood, straightening her back'),
('Relishing rejection. Filling with anger decoupled from a linguistic structure.
Her spiritual ideal was not really compassion', 'She saw her heart materialize
in front of her. From the median nerve center and solar plexus, down the spine,
a burning path of fire affixed a seal in front of him. She breathed from six dif-
ferent places. "To be a Christian is to act for others. The body hardens, because
the other is sovereign." She had said. The vision of the fire walled her off from
others. She wanted to tell her father what touched her')
;
```

MAURE COISE 41

```sql
CREATE TABLE dbo.PerfectNothing
(TheFormOfTheLived varchar(35) NOT NULL PRIMARY KEY,
HardeningTheBodyIntoStone varchar(40) NOT NULL
);


INSERT INTO dbo.PerfectNothing (TheFormOfTheLived, HardeningTheBodyIntoStone)
VALUES
```

('Like the harmonizing of tones, breaking hydrogen and oxygen and reuniting
them., magnetic and electric. In a note held, severing one', 'Bronwen was sad-
dened, thinking of her 33rd birthday. So far, yet close. She wanted a child then. Born
on March 22nd. Every movement she made impacted their future. Nourishing. She
forgot all else'),
('Breathing in 4/5th oxygen and 1/5th nitrogen. Slowly, a venous flow became
arterial. She smelled a fragrance, sweeter than honeysuckle, germination itself. The
note, 300,000 vibrations per second, constituted another realm, an elevated sense.
The flute, rebec, bagpipe, ocarinas shortened and lengthened wavelengths', 'As a
communication with an invisible order of beings; that influenced her, pre-cognitive-
ly, in sense modulation, analogous to major or minor tones'),
('The wind blew through the instruments. ', ' She wanted them to love her, to mani-
fest in physiognomy, the F tone, circular overlapping waves, repeating 300 times; an
amplitude'),
('In Matthew 18, Peter asks Christ how to forgive. Christ gives the parable of
counting servants. When one couldn't pay, they promised to worship their master
and were forgiven their debt', 'Then, in 24, on the Mount of Olives, the beginning
of sorrow, the abomination of desolation, stand on a holy place. For when the stars
fall, there will be two in the fields and only one shall be taken')
('And then, 25, ten women wait for the groom, only five bring oil for their lamps',
'Paul in Romans 8, to walk after the spirit, we are debtors. To bear witness to the
coming blessing')
;

```
CREATE TABLE dbo.NualaPrays
(
DeterminedByChildhoodData varchar(400) NOT NULL PRIMARY KEY,
AcquiredLanguage varchar(500) NOT NULL
);

INSERT INTO dbo. NualaPrays (DeterminedByChildhoodData, AcquiredLanguage)
VALUES ('Dedication was her death knell. She wasted away in idleness, unable
to observe the form of her own thinking. If she had a notion of order, she
stuck to it, overriding all else', 'In her subconscious, and in her conscious sense
expectation automatized, she willed to act differently, and to learn to observe
her conditions'),
('The Church Fathers, she believed, were merciful. They knew she had faltered in
her teenage years. She identified with her frail body', 'She ignored her electro-
magnetic field. She did not think about gravity'),
('The frail body was a block to observing displacement. She shirked any sense of
duty', 'Egotism is the name for her overwhelming suggestibility')
;
```

```sql
CREATE TABLE dbo.SixDemonVisitations
(
Apollo varchar(400) NOT NULL PRIMARY KEY,
Cheng varchar(220) NOT NULL,
House varchar(300) NOT NULL,
SweatAndFoul varchar(400) NOT NULL,
Heat varchar(220) NOT NULL,
Six varchar(300) NOT NULL
);

INSERT INTO dbo. SixDemonVisitations (Apollo, Cheng, House, SweatAndFoul, Heat,
Six)
VALUES
('Apollo bet Nuala she could maintain good conscience while stealing money from
her parens. She drained their savings.  Got used to living in luxury, siphoning from
their bank account. A flow from one bank account to another', 'Chen taught to
principles, time and idiocy. They taught the construction of a drain pump to gener-
ate an alternative electromagnetism, misaligning her hips', 'House convinced her of
social decay. And that slave morality was a fixation', 'Sweat and Foul convinced her
to study sexuality, actualizing a crust of hate through masturbation', 'Heat shift-
ed her pyhysiology further, inititating her into an ideal society of spiritual entities
following the principles of depravity, self-satisfaction, destruction, freedom from
nature, concealing, enjoying what they don't deserve, and being what they are
not. To repress sexual shame, she turned to drugs', 'Six fused Nuala's haughtiness
with a rejection of health. She fused her interest in the Church with Americanism.
Embraced the crusades in Iraq, Afghanistan, and also Pakistan')
;
```

```sql
CREATE TABLE dbo.HarmonicIntervals
(EmbodyingAWarlikeCharacteristicBetweenIdiocyAndCells varchar(500) NOT
NULL PRIMARY KEY,
SheInventsAbstinence varchar(700) NOT NULL
);


INSERT INTO dbo.HarmonicIntervals(EmbodyingAWarlikeCharacteristicBetweenI-
diocyAndCells, SheInventsAbstinence)
VALUES
('In her studies, in automatic writing, Nuala discovers an instrument with 103
strings and an echo chamber that generates 17 distinct whole tones. Moving
from G to B to G to C to B to F. Using an iron bar to halve the length of each
string blends consonance. With just two notes, this instrument could change the
texture of her skin', 'Meanwhile, Bronwen fell in love with another woman'),
('Nuala saw the need to attend to death, to develop a death memory.', 'The col-
onization her ancestors perpetrated were so often acts of love. Men scrambling
by any measure to pay off debts and give their lovers luxurious lives'),
('Christianity prepared her for alienation, for racism.', 'She found a non-mechan-
ical energy, a weakness. She existed through others' words. She lacked direct
emotional encounters. Others owned her, only participating in legion desires.
But to attend to the tensions of dismemberment she needed to be available'),
('Heightening sensitivity required maintenance', 'She bypassed mechanization
by computer addiction. Wasting what could have been rest.')
;
```

```sql
CREATE TABLE dbo.ContinuityAndContinuum
(
SheIsToldToMoveToTheCountry varchar(400) NOT NULL PRIMARY KEY,
SheIsToldToEatFreshDairy varchar(80) NOT NULL,
InConneticutGraniteWasARemainderFromTheIceAge varchar(250) NOT NULL,
ThreadedThroughHerLifeWasASecondTimeline varchar(225) NOT NULL
);

INSERT INTO dbo.ContinuityAndContinuum (SheIsToldToMoveToTheCountry, SheIs-
ToldToEatFreshDairy, InConneticutGraniteWasARemainderFromTheIceAge, Thread-
edThroughHerLifeWasASecondTimeline)
VALUES
('In a moment she felt the space of her body', 'Intensity formed a second ground,
stretching out to the sun', 'Hidden in the woods or on the beach', 'Nuala didn't
speak much because she could hardly remember the word she had started pro-
nouncing by the end of it')
;
```

```
CREATE TABLE dbo.TalkingIsAutomatic
(
EnglishWasImplanted varchar(900) NOT NULL PRIMARY KEY
ToDeflateOrBurnAwayIdiomaticPatternsWasItselfADefenseMechanism varchar(540)
NOT NULL
);


INSERT INTO dbo.TalkingIsAutomatic (EnglishWasImplanted, ToDeflateOrBurnAway-
IdiomaticPatternsWasItselfADefenseMechanism')
VALUES
('The laws of relativity might offer an ability to pay', 'Just as a broken planetary
fragment becomes a satellite, so the orbit sexuates')
;
```

```sql
CREATE TABLE dbo.SixDemonVisitations2
(
AnInterventionToAvoidLaboringForMoney varchar(70) NOT NULL PRIMARY KEY
RuiningTheCenteringOfGravity varchar(45) NOT NULL,
StopGoingToChurch varchar(85) NOT NULL
StudyEgypt varchar(70) NOT NULL
StudyMesopotamia varchar(45) NOT NULL,
BecomeShameless varchar(85) NOT NULL

);

INSERT INTO dbo.SixDemonVisitations2 (AnInterventionToAvoidLaboringForMoney,
RuiningTheCenteringOfGravity, StopGoingToChurch, StudyEgypt, StudyMesopota-
mia, BecomeShameless)
VALUES
```

('Phenomenal characteristics, most impactful to an experience of time are anode-di-
ode', 'Nuala doubled the proportionality.', 'She had her own moral metaphysics of
solitude', 'Time sped up', 'She was obsessed', 'She couldn't pay'),
('Her instincts became pure guilt. Her emotional regulations became purely me-
chanical. She stuffed herself with information. Crystallized in the English language.
She transformed physically Her blood vessels dilated. She was a circuit, sealed like a
mummy. Submitting to suggestion. She lived in a religious war. America against the
Islamicate. Christ was the model ruler.', 'In music, a note could float long enough to
hear melodies in it. A uniform current, with a number of vibrations, the amperage
could be accumulated and condensed to facilitate metastases. She was bound to
Christian sexuality. She built a Solomonic pillar from her subconscious defining her
station as transgression, crystallizing her inner tyrant. She gave up everything for
Apollo and Cheng, for a presence at the edge, longing to misalign, to receive mes-
sages in the vibratory', 'She was initiated into measuring value. She was nowhere to
be found. At home, she called for the demonic help. The impression was lost when it
was conceived. She could only observe the insufficiency of her body-perception. She
struggled to be available. They came in flashes. A functional contact with an intel-
ligence, and she followed her intuitions blindly. It was different from suggestibility
because of an inner tonus. The continuity of tensing and relaxing was defeasible.
Measuring, delimiting her will, to play a role for the will. Engaging in the current
of the Church was responsible. The reciprocity of exchanges brought awareness
of conditions, finding the right tempo and posture. Nuala's chest tightened. She
wanted to observe the continuity of two unknown variables. Abstracting her living
material', 'These visits, 1, 2, 3, 2, 1, intensified. Blending into 4 by way of 5 and 6.
Opening her to a quality', 'The shift from Sweat and Foul to Heat was an attuning

to reactive friction. She was sucking a new quality, galvanizing a voltage. She could only feel her body mass. Cycling, circulating arms and legs. She was a vessel for the making of a new body. She was the observation of the failure of this, a lack of effort. Christianity failed her', 'She rejected conscience. She couldn't make a new body to pay for her body. She couldn't unite to stay in front of her inability. What could she do if there was no Nuala? She was a puppet of the six demons. She affirmed it. She liked it because it made her feel good. Letting others make her decisions and desires')

;

```sql
CREATE TABLE dbo.InTheNameOfTheFatherTheSonAndTheHolySpirit
(
Calm varchar(45) NOT NULL PRIMARY KEY,
MakingInformationOutOfData varchar(40) NOT NULL,
HerDemonologyProducedAVacuum varchar(150) NOT NULL
);

INSERT INTO dbo. InTheNameOfTheFatherTheSonAndTheHolySpirit (Calm, Making-
InformationOutOfData, HerDemonologyProducedAVacuum)
VALUES
('Constructing a vessel for life maintenance... she nearly died at birth, she had to
be taken from her mother in the hospital immediately, for a whole week', 'It took
nearly all of her energy to connect her fragmented parts. Sexual repression made
it easier', 'She wrote freely, ideating freely, without any sense of duty. Through
successive fractioning of light and dark, she alternated infinitesimal calculus and
subjunctive love framed as amplitude. She created an alternative to the Church,
theosophical narcissism'),
('Her soul striving for beyond. She established an order whose merit was bound
to the individual', 'This compelled her to hate society even more. Driven by fear of
exposure', 'Her cerebral nerve ganglia crystallized passivity in relation to an associa-
tive flow.'),
('She developed two tempos of blood circulation', 'She chose to concentrate on
one', 'Her attempt, guilt ridden, organized degrees of power, towards attaining a
station. The death drive denies differentiation, and is reducible to a fear of nuisanc-
es. Driven by ignorance of bodily impressions')
;
```

```
CREATE TABLE dbo.SixDemonVisitations3
(
PreserveTheWolf varchar(20) NOT NULL PRIMARY KEY,
ImproviseAMelody varchar(35) NOT NULL
Soul varchar(20) NOT NULL,
Unwhole varchar(35) NOT NULL
VibratoryPressures varchar(20) NOT NULL,
Taxation varchar(35) NOT NULL
);


INSERT INTO dbo.SixDemonVisitations3 (PreserveTheWolf, ImproviseAMelody,
Soul, Unwhole, VibratoryPressures, Taxation)
VALUES
('Her parents reach financial stability gradually, slowly. It was too hard for her.
She had to travel up river for wisdom. Spatial know-how took plenty of money.
She needed to avoid the swindle of careerism. What was the difference between
money stolen and earned? Nothing. The self is the one who has the money',
'There are limits to knowledge, the structure of thinking, as scale sensitivity.
Intervals reflected in harmonies pass through half tones. To calculate a field of
conception, the mechanisms of purposeless associations build the capacities
of a meaningful perspective. Conditions for plurality, ungoverned, she couldn't
muster the energy to do the smallest thing. Subjective associations are propor-
tional, fast/slow or long/short, and shaped by inheritance. Inhaling/exhaling.
Nuala played many roles, not just the ones that suited her, by chance. She made
an effort to consider the quartertones. Like glue. To make decisions to love'
'She wanted to be Bronwen's servant. The orbit of fragments needed ever more
laziness. To preserve the idea of solitude, she used deception. She wanted to
return to the womb. She didn't care when Bronwen fell in love with someone
else. She could retreat to vain jealousy. The Church had given her the symbolic
framework. She believed she possessed Bronwen. Nothing else mattered. In
her inner sanctum, she could control the ebb and flow of a pulse', 'Summoning
a physical regimen, she exercised her abilities in writing mystical nonsense',
'Delimiting consciousness to negate consciousness, she survived the flood by an
overwhelming foundation of blood', 'She disliked Bronwen's new lover. From an
epigenetic lens, the familial struggle might be analyzed as Nuala's cultivation of
a public memory')
;
```

```sql
CREATE TABLE dbo.AnImpressionOfValueThroughAccretion
(
WorldParts varchar(45) NOT NULL PRIMARY KEY,
TrickedIntoASenseOfSelf varchar(40) NOT NULL,
AtTheBrink varchar(150) NOT NULL
);

INSERT INTO dbo.AnImpressionOfValueThroughAccretion (WorldParts, TrickedIntoA-
SenseOfSelf, AtTheBrink)
VALUES
('The power to direct an energy current depends on the velocity of attention. Guid-
ed by others, Nuala, passively worked on radiography in near complete isolation
to avoid others radiaion. This initiation was led by gluttony', 'For three months, she
communed with her six demons, passing through three stages of impulses. First,
what can I do, what do I want to do, and what can I do that I want to do. Can is
here related to the agglomeration of motor nerve nodes in spine, and want with the
sympathetic nerve nodes', 'She attended to this, in sense and feeling, as an acquisi-
tion, as preparation to actualize in interactions, in a group the sharing of exercises')
;
```

```
CREATE TABLE dbo.ThreePhases
(
2000 varchar(45) NOT NULL PRIMARY KEY,
2002 varchar(40) NOT NULL,
2008 varchar(150) NOT NULL
);
```

```
INSERT INTO dbo. ThreePhases (2000, 2002, 2008)
VALUES
```
('Outer impressions characterizing Nuala are implanted from outside, in the form of ages 1 to 8', 'Outer perception functionally linked to inherited reflexes', 'Outer impressions and outer perception are linked as voluntary contact of contemplation and use, intention contingent on interaction'),
('The danger of conflating sense and feeling is a blockage of expression and experience. To mourn her own death, she lazily decided she needed a soul. To blend inner and outer as affine relation and social reciprocity. to subdivide proportions of duration and atmosphere. The latter internal, in proportion to the subdivision of affirmation and negation of internalization and externalization. Life, as neutralizing, as mourning, might connect through disconnecting pseudo-connections. The first nine years concretized this.', 'Then, the biological self, Nuala, codifies the meaning of the sameness of Nuala, as the direction of Nuala's likes. This was malformed because of the continuous confusion of sensation and emotion. So, she struggled in generating atmospheric conditions.', 'These pivots were geolocated in New Haven, first in two visits. Then, moving there, the crystallizing of other-consciousness as a reception of inner/outer. She made the mistake of treating her demons as outside. She was addicted to information. Inventing the fantasy of an exterior to which she could be passive. The pain itself was analogous to inner and outer. To touch this third was enough to shatter, so she constructed an illusion of touch, decoupling "I can want" from action')
;

```sql
CREATE TABLE dbo.BronwenIsARealist
(
TheVeridicalityOfSensingAndFeelingIsMoreThanVerbal varchar(80) NOT NULL
PRIMARY KEY,
TheExistentCertaintyOfCommonSenseIsNumericalObjectivity varchar(150) NOT
NULL
);
```

INSERT INTO dbo.BronwenIsARealist (TheVeridicalityOfSensingAndFeelingIsMore-
ThanVerbal, TheExistentCertaintyOfCommonSenseIsNumericalObjectivity)
VALUES ('The whole is a concomitance of constituent parts ', 'Nuala was more of a
nominalist, stopping at, "this seems like X to me." Bronwen didn't find it unneces-
sary to say that was precisely, "this is X."'),
('Bronwen was interested in types. To say, in subjective conditions, a universal,
such as touch, was inherited through participation, not as an abstract entity, but a
material feature of types of participation. Touch is located in moments and instants.
In predicative language, adjective and adverb', 'Nuala focused on the role of the
locator, the origin of the locative exertion. In xRy, x and y belong to R. This was
foundational for modus pollens, if x then y. R could be subject, but not conscious-
ness. Further, personhood was made up of what it was not, i.e. gut bacteria. Since
locator was merely a designation of aggregates, an intermediation without sub-
stance or stability, then representational capacities were irrelevant to sharing public
spaces. Saying, "I seem to have a sense or feeling" might categorize an occurrence
but is not propositional. As a person, one might delimit sense or feeling virtually,
as a hypothetical. But even then, Nuala thought it was only through exclusion,
discriminating components, what is not sensed or felt, awareness of particularity
determining a whole apprehension is inferred as a srquence grasped as a temporal
extension of a mental episode externalizing a spatial discrimination through imag-
ining and thereby consummating the location. This is not subjective agency as much
as knowing according to a convention in a level of negation. Bronwen had no way
of arguing with this idealist view. Even if she said I have nothing, I want nothing,
I still am, I eat, there is content and a causal structure by which she acts. Even if
she was indifferent she still supposed her acting. Nuala denied actors. If her hand
moved, it didn't matter if it was because of biological factors or an unknown force.
At the atomic level conceptual attachments were impossible'),
('"Why is my hand moving" always loops back to fear of bondage to experience.
Inseparable from the subject-predicate-object triplet. To accumulate and transfer
words about the impression, converting hypotheticals divides the discrimination of
time and act as a codependent appellation. Discrete units sequenced in perspec-
tives toward acquisition. This is effort', 'For Nuala, combating nihilistic tendencies

called for affirming double negation, a dynamic designation of imaginal procedural orientation, discriminating others' discrimination, inhering nothing, in neither effort nor evidence. Witnessing awareness of nothing, as codependence of conditions and conventions. The nothing of concrete particulars, as aspect of ability to cognize classifiers binds mental episodes to apprehension's forcefulness. Rites are attained through propriety. Nuala saw cataloguing as lived ideal of imagining dependencies as more or less consummate to nothing. Opening locativity'),

('Bronwen saw this as leading directly to authoritarianism. But, what doesn't. It was negative mysticism. That linguistic mediation could be carved out to reach the epistemological commitments. Nuala spent all her time writing about these philosophical problems. She must have been abused as a child. She was obsessed with pronomial becoming. So afraid of the molecular oscillations needed to direct a current. She was so afraid of sexual education. Her thoughts seemed to become more and more vague and meandering', 'But everyday she still got coffee and a croissant. Nuala walked down the stairs, past the chipped paint. But then, they'd spend less time together. Nuala blamed Bronwen for everything. The loosening links of her mental wandering forced them to eat more and more takeout. She detached from her environment and from experience, playing only with shifting words. Nuala wanted to control the sound of her voice. She was so afraid of the sonic quality of Bronwen's voice. She was Bronwen's caretaker and wished for no other social role. Her philosophical concerns were an excuse to reach a velocity. She didn't have to earn anything.')

;

```
CREATE TABLE dbo.HerBlackTeachersWouldHaveBeenAppalledAtHerLaziness
(
WealthAccumulatedThroughColonization varchar(40) NOT NULL PRIMARY KEY,
NeverChallenged varchar(20) NOT NULL,
SheDidNotKeepHerDemonsClose varchar(20) NOT NULL
);


INSERT INTO dbo.HerBlackTeachersWouldHaveBeenAppalledAtHerLaziness
(WealthAccumulatedThroughColonization, NeverChallenged, SheDidNotKeepHer-
DemonsClose)
VALUES
```

('Nuala wanted to control others' speech. Her parents were teachers. She didn't just corrct grammar. She wanted absolute quiet, Her freedom depended on it', 'She only interacted with white people', 'As a child, she once asked her mom, who was that one really smart black person? She was thinking of W.E.B. DuBois.'),

('Nuala fell into the white supremacist occult because her parents had prepared her for it. She embraced an outsider role institutionally supported. She was never punished', 'Her antisocial belief was on the uniqueness of her hate', 'She was pre-pared to be warped by nationalism'),

('Her easy living hurt others. For one example, gentrifying her New Haven neigh-borhood', 'Was it psychic revenge for being a minority in a black public school. For getting picked on?', 'She did not want to engage'),

('She didn't know how to communicate. She assumed black people didn't want to talk to her', 'What creative accomplishments would have triggered her to be excited enough to reach out?', 'She just wanted to do what she wanted. Black etiquette had too many rules'),

('She was so slow. It took so much time for her to reach a basic level of comfort.', 'She never hung out with black kids after school, but she had hung out with other white kids', 'What reinforced this?'),

('One reason was that the black students were too hygienic for her. She did not like the smell of fluoride mouthwash', 'She appropriated supernatural whiteness. She listened to a lot of black music. But, she also saw black music in aesthetic levels. And the dominant American corporatism of black music she held in disdain', 'She associated violence more as by then to black people. The only time she ever felt afraid was when she thought she didn't get into a magnet middle school that would have taken her away from the black public school to suffer the violence of black teenagers'),

('She didn't delve into the black intelligence she experienced in elementary school, she didn't respect it. She ran away', 'She possessed space', 'She did not know how to resist her empowerment by way of colonization. She did not dismantle her position as a know it all'),

('To take a risk to listen, to break down what she thinks she is, and stay in front of this while interacting', 'Breaking the associative flow takes strength. Nuala didn't have it. She was defensive. Stunned. She'd drop out', 'Her solitude took resources. She filtered everything through Bronwen. Nuala's identification with femininity was bound to a disidentification with black people. For fear of being an effeminite boy in a black public school.')

('As a moral ideal, Afrocentrism might be cultivated, as listening with care. To dismantle biases in discipline and punishment, in the security of solitude', 'She had to divest in engagement with white supremacist material. Including the Church.', 'Then she might learn to meditate on her childhood black influences, to make amends with internalized hate. Why had she centered on the white occult influence? Out of respect for silence? She had repressed the black teachings on etiquette she had learned to make use of the rebel-victim role')

;

```
CREATE VIEW Publishing
AS
SELECT SheWasPersecuted, TheVeridicalityOfSensingAndFeelingIsMoreThanVerbal,
TheExistentCertaintyOfCommonSenseIsNumericalObjectivity
FROM dbo.AnythingNualaDidWouldGoWrong et
JOIN dbo.BronwenIsARealist e
ON et.SheWasPerscuted = e.SheWasPerscuted;
GO
```

```
CREATE VIEW DataStorage
AS
SELECT InTheTriadicMediationOfConnectionAndConditions, TranslatingInitiate-
sAnInterpretation, ImproviseAMelody
FROM dbo. NualaLookedForStillness et
JOIN dbo. SixDemonVisitations3e
ON et. InTheTriadicMediationOfConnectionAndConditions = e. InTheTriadicMe-
diationOfConnectionAndConditions;
GO
```

```sql
CREATE VIEW DataStorage2
AS
SELECT l. SheDoesNotWantToBeSeen, SheDidn'tKnowTheNamesOfThePieces, l.
SheDidNotKeepHerDemonsClose
FROM dbo. NualaAtTheConcert b
JOIN dbo. TheConcertHasPedagogicalValue l
ON b. SheDoesNotWantToBeSeen = l. SheDoesNotWantToBeSeen
JOIN dbo. HerBlackTeachersWouldHaveBeenAppalledAtHerLaziness e
ON l. SheDidNotKeepHerDemonsClose = e. SheDidNotKeepHerDemonsClose;
GO
```

Load data

```
library(Real)
data(used in terms of knowledge and being a restriction on an argument to
determine acceptance)

library(data.table)
MyFeetDoNotExist <- data.table(reconciling a vision and its visuals)
```

Preliminary plots of the data

```
scatter_1 <- ggplot(EyesGazingOut, aes(x=MoreThanTheEyeDelimiting, y=Evi-
dencingFallaciousInferences)) +
  geom_jitter(aes(color=ultimately inexistent and conventionally illusory))+
  labs(Title="Autonomous Inferences",
     x="conditioned",
     y="unconditioned")
print(scatter_1)

scatter_2 <- ggplot(LogicalRelations, aes(x=DescriptionOfContradiction, y=Cor-
rectPropositions)) +
  geom_jitter(aes(color=Real))+
  labs(Title="Categorization",
     x="EffectsOfQualities",
     y="CollectiveEffect")
print(scatter_2)
```

Regression

```
multivariate_continuous <- lm(ANewFoot~CenterFoot + Effect + CausedBy-
FeetQualities, data=CenterFootQualities)
summary(multivariate_continuous)
```

Plot prediction

```
InheringFromSubstratumDirectionalQualities[, predictedACentralQuality:= pre-
dict(multivariate_continuous, data=CenterFootQualities)]
```

```
ggplot(DyadicOntogenesis, aes(x=EyingQualities)) +
  geom_point(aes(y=Cognizing), alpha=0.7) +
  geom_line(aes(y=predictedLessIllustrationThanMetaphor), size=1) +
  labs(title="Center Foot Has Causal and Noncausal Origins",
      x="relation of right and left foot",
      y="separation of center from conjunction of right and left foot")

ggplot(ThereIsNoHalfCenterFoot, aes(x=SeparationOfQualities)) +
  geom_point(aes(y=DestructionOfPreexistingApplicationsOfCombination), al-
pha=0.7) +
  geom_line(aes(y=predictedSelfSuspended), size=1) +
  labs(title="Reasoning Applied",
      x="Whole",
      y="Parts")
```

3

import pandas as pd
df = pd.read_csv("I've Come To This Forest, To Listen To The Aurora Australis
(Talking, on video, on the phone, I am told', 'Audible, at least, by some defini-
tions of the word audible, auroral activity is solar plasma that has been warped
by ionospheric electromagnetic activity', 'I am supported', 'Ionized particles
collude with high altitude atoms', 'Walking into the forest', 'Most arrive here
by mistake, but I have come willingly', 'Children command animal armies', 'This
place is born of VLF waves', 'Children run through the forest', 'The sky glows
with the residual luminosity of stable pulsations'), The Electron Cyclotron Maser
(I Knock On The Door, I Record Periodicity, I Leave ('I failed', 'Monitoring the
expanding pitch angle distribution of motion characteristics', 'I am at my desk',
'Preciptating into ionospheric parameters', 'I want to work', 'I withdraw my
whip antennae', 'My invention was', 'Radio signals fall in pitch from 10,000 to
200 Hz ', 'It's a kind of posession')), Control Of The Dynamic Of Inner And Outer
Radiation Belts (ItIsGrowing, ItIsNotHuman ('Things are bad', 'This old elongat-
ed doughnut shaped field has holes at the poles', 'Research continues on the
subconscious', 'I've followed the trail for miles only to arrive at a question', 'An-
tipathic coding seems impossible, same for sympathetic', 'There are magnitudes
of fluxes of energetic particles, but what is their mechanism of precipitation and
how does it vary as a function'))")

df

df.sort_values(by=" Looking At It (It Is Changing Colors, Ionospheric Effects
Of Relativistic Electron Precipitation, I See It Glowing, A Spread Of Intensities
('In the forest, we look at each other', 'Models of time sequences allow agents
to innovate', 'Thinking, even when looking is a sin', 'Detection of length and
time-scale allow micro/macro analysis to build a variety of levels of organiza-
tion, a variety of perspectives', 'We are doomed to be embodied, that stands
in the way of being with another', 'Inferential activity encodes intervals as time
series', 'Why did you leave', 'I'd signed up last week', 'What holds us together',
'I've come to study behavior and simply describe these behaviors', 'Can one be
oneself', 'I image, not a characteristic duration or size, but how, for any given
duration there are five times fewer patches that last twice as long and five times
more patches that last half as long', 'Do we believe in another's pain', 'Spatial
mapping and the coordination of groups relate manifolds of grid cells across
the entorhinal cortex', 'Feeding vitamins to possession, hunger', 'Distances,

integrating firing patterns', 'As if this were still Earth', 'Interferences relate place fields, the flow of time through the concept of number', 'Spectograms turning', 'Gravity-inertia and its electromagnetic limits, singularities controlled by geodesics, external frames of reference expressed as amplitudes, to which the internal frame is as continuous as space-time')), It is Raining (Calling, How To Get Magnetic Disturbances From A Peak Current Or From An Arbitrary Threshold ('Running', 'Probability densities follows power laws', 'Passed out', 'I was invited here', 'Using a syringe', 'To demonstrate the substorm components', 'I felt you and you were nothing like I imagined', 'Global scale energy release allows deterministic description', 'Another you appears', 'The convection measure of the near Gaussian distribution differs spatial separation', 'Seeing someone recognized, I call the name', 'The re-scaled power law of velocity fluctuation, turbulence, percolation, needs exponential truncation')), Panic (She Helps Coordinate Recording VLF, I Do Not Know You, Predicting Waiting Times ('Takes a drink', 'No human can hear radio waves from 100-10,000 cycles per second (0.110 kHz)', 'We pick and choose what we want of technologies', 'Recording the ducts of solar wind, disperesed in the magnetic field', 'I don't know what is happening, but it is a global phenomena', 'To study time versus frequency components', 'For some, it is like displacement', 'Monitoring electromagnetic impulses with VLF', 'Others begin to feel each other totally', 'Wave-guide dispersion caught in lines stretching to the poles', 'Attract a stranger and kiss', 'Like sferics', 'Like a virus', 'Alternate current power lines hum', 'A special effect'))")

df.describe

df.iloc("Tracking Magnetic Conditions By Radio (Have You Been In Love, Modeling Pulsations With Pink And White Noise, We Begin To Relax ('She wasn't getting my definitions of the power law in the interactions between Earth and sun, and that was my fault', 'Interconnections, our machines look at', 'I'd signed up with the wrong definitions', 'Vague, I didn't think it would work', 'With her, the larger point was that planetary science doesn't just serve complexity', 'What am I thinking', 'It is driven by complexification, in part', 'Alcohol, pour a drink, the effect is universal', 'The force of an interruption between production and reproductio'), What Is The Source Of The Radiation(The Character Of Time, We Are Victims ('Tuning to reception, signals, in an extended situating of state and correlation length', 'We won't find the source', 'We can direct the radiation', 'Contradictory effects', 'We aren't the only ones set up here, on this burial mound', 'I'm writing a letter, lighting a cigarette')), Signal Distribution At Very Low Frequencies, Describing the noise's effect on future memory")

df.set_index("Reactions To The Waves(First Creative Feeling Then Sexual Ecstasy,

Absorbing Radiation ('The passed out one wakes up', 'Today it looks like we will have to launch certain animals into space to follow the magnetic field for their dances and routes', 'It is a jelly', 'Driving animals into extinction', 'It is multi-plicative, subjective', 'Threatening', 'Looking at possession', 'We'd spent some time analyzing two completely modeled auroral sequences', 'It smells like urine', 'We were looking for the time of the most audible sound, and we knew what to listen for in order to find it')) (AlgebraicLogic, ThereAreNoLies, 1sAnd0sInBrains 'There's no more need', 'Axioms of natural numbers', 'See the time scales', 'Translating the magnetic field into sound', 'Local disturbances', 'Mingling communication', 'The screen shows dots and dashes', 'Listening to the produc-tion of our encoded field of radio waves', 'A model of the universe with a crack in the spectrogram, I see a face in it')) Worshipping The Idea Of Value (Scream-ing, Competition ('I need help', 'Cognizing numeracy, a general magnitude', 'Controlling the radiations in insanity, hopeless', 'Language is interdependent, a consequence of interaction', 'We need proper administration', 'Scientists are entitled to empirical truth because of the correspondence bewteen a notion and a picture of reliable interaction'))")

df.shape

df.link

df.drop_duplicates

%matplotlib inline
df.plot()

%matplotlib inline
df."Belief In Natural Order (Lost Recordings, Communization, Nameless, Awakening ('Not integrating', 'Is this the problem', 'Not knowing, innocent', 'Accosted', 'Saying no to artifice, because there is too much distance', 'Cool', 'We study the space of the map', 'What happened', 'Comparing n-paths with n-equivalences', 'Evolving', 'Raising the dimension to n+1', 'Seeing faces every-where', 'Mapping cresponding frames of reference', 'Buzzing from the mon-itor', 'Inverting transformations to discern invariant properties from which we predicate anew', 'Disappear, the other is still lying down', 'The cognitive subject constitutes a history, compressing a model into a prediction pattern', 'It seems as though we've lost it', 'Affirming the method of reduction', 'I'm not well')), I Am Death I Have Been Dead For Days, Logical Depth ('Have I been with a ghost', 'The consuming factor suggests similarity', 'I believe the source has been

been discovered', 'As we recognize predators', 'A stopped historical flow', 'Unmaking conditions of action', 'And you are ready to go public to show it', 'Recordings, recored in fear, from a need to handle a concept', 'No one will appreciate', 'Not emphasizing', 'Alone, taking a drink', 'We don't produce concepts')), Uncontrollable Ghosts Appear Everywhere (Provoking The Name Of Sense, No One Knows What To Do, Specific Living Phenomena Establish Geometries ('I want to hold you again and ask you, why is time still', 'According to the reciprocal determination of causal structures', 'Squinting, looking at the data, this will change the climate', 'Between proof and construction there is a gap', 'Carbon dioxide balance is being destroyed at a greater rate than human global warming', 'Cognition and digital modeling follows a geodesic', 'Individuality precluded a sign', 'Modeling minimal computations for finite description', 'I believe, she said, that to destroy the soul would be un-Christian', 'The causal hierarchy of agency, generated out of finite resources, utilizes inductive inference for recognition', 'Fate is sealed', 'Local interactions, irreversible, such that tensegrity constructs properties of invariance might be categorized', 'In copper wiring', 'Contingencies of living interfaces', 'Why speak when you can read my mind, yes, that is the right question, I'm wrong to continue'))".plot()

Inside the Castle